SUPPLEMENT

International Music Publications Limited

NB pages 2 & 3 in the FLUTE and CLARINET books can be played together in 3rds.

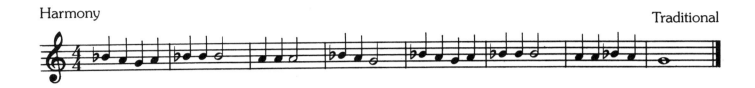

Merrily we roll along

Harmony

Traditional

Au clair de la lune

Harmony

Traditional

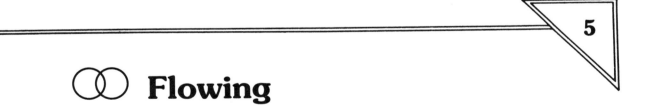

Flowing

Harmony

Walking

Harmony

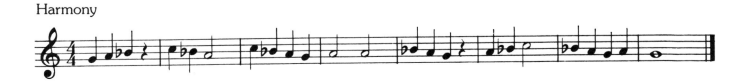

One man and his dog

Harmony

Traditional

Go and tell aunt Rhody

Unison

Traditional

Skip to my Lou

Harmony

Traditional

soft

The cuckoo

Harmony

EDWARD DUCKETT

Fine

loud

D.C. al Fine

soft

Rule Britannia

THOMAS AUGUSTINE ARNE
(1710–1778)

Unison

Rigaudon

Unison   ■ *Rigaudon* for Clarinet Unison on page 29 in the CLARINET book.   HENRY PURCELL
(1659–1695)

(Opt.)

Ode to joy

LUDWIG VAN BEETHOVEN
(1770–1827)

Unison

Semiquaver study

Pomp and Circumstance March No.1

EDWARD ELGAR
(1857–1934)

Star Wars main theme

■ *Star Wars* for Clarinet Unison on page 52 in the CLARINET book.

JOHN WILLIAMS

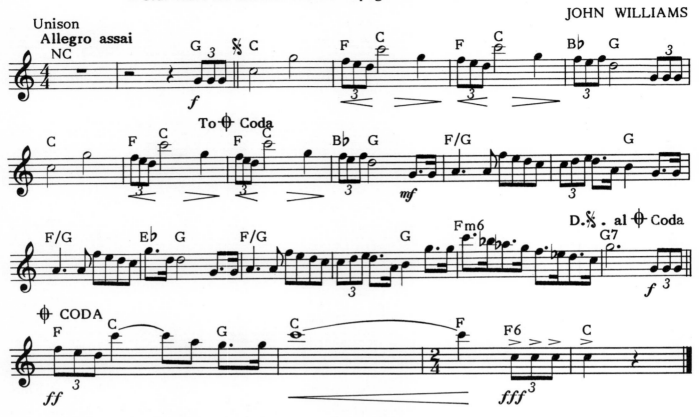

Lasst uns erfreuen

Traditional

Over the rainbow

Words by E.Y. HARBURG
Music by HAROLD ARLEN

Unison

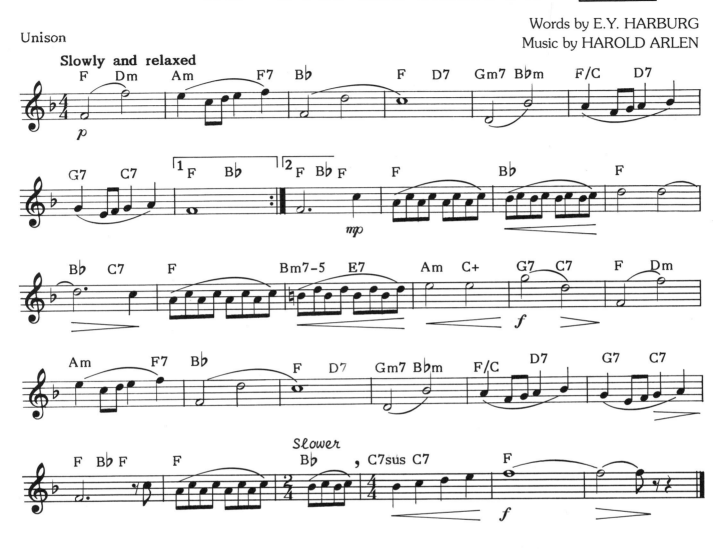

FLUTE

TEAM WOODWIND

CORMAC LOANE and RICHARD DUCKETT

4·95.

International Music Publications Limited

Introduction

The TEAM WOODWIND series has been designed to meet the needs of young wind players everywhere, whether lessons are given individually, in groups or in the classroom.

Musical variety

Each book contains a wide variety of musical styles, from the Baroque and Classical eras to film, folk, jazz and Latin American. In addition there are original pieces and studies, technical exercises and scales, progressing from the beginner stage to approximately Grade IV standard of the *Associated Board of the Royal Schools of Music*. Furthermore TEAM WOODWIND offers material suitable for mixed wind ensemble as well as solos with piano accompaniment.

Ensemble pieces

All TEAM WOODWIND books contain corresponding pages of music which can be played together in harmony. Beginners are thus given early ensemble experience and the opportunity to share lessons with other players, whether they play treble or bass clef, B flat, C or E flat pitched instruments, or even guitar or keyboards.

The ensemble material in the TEAM WOODWIND series integrates with the same material in TEAM BRASS and thus offers exciting possibilities for mixed instrumental lessons, concerts and assemblies.

Study options

The TEAM WOODWIND series is not a 'method'. It is a selection of primer music from which the teacher can select a suitably graded course for each pupil. This allows for variation in concentration threshold and tempo of progression. There are also several choices of progressive path the pupil can follow. Study options appear at the foot of appropriate pages.

GCSE skills

In addition to fostering musical literacy, Rhythm Grids and Play By Ear lines provide early opportunities for composition and improvisation. This aspect of TEAM WOODWIND can be a useful starting point for these elements in the GCSE examination course now followed in many secondary schools.

Comprehensive notes on the use of this series, scores of ensemble pieces and piano accompaniments are given in the ACCOMPANIMENTS book.

Team Woodwind Ensemble

TEAM WOODWIND ensemble material has been specially written so that it can be played by almost any combination of wind instruments that the teacher is likely to encounter. The pieces are basically for duet, to which can be added independent (and inessential) third and fourth parts if required.

TEAM WOODWIND for FLUTE includes fifteen flute duets. Related 3rd ensemble parts for Clarinet in B flat and C appear in the Supplement to the CLARINET book.

This book also contains ensemble material relating to the duets in TEAM WOODWIND for CLARINET. Relevant parts to the clarinet duets appear on the same numbered pages in all TEAM WOODWIND books, e.g. parts relating to *German tune* (clarinet duet) appear on page 14 in all books. Also, the B flat ensemble material integrates fully with the ensemble material in the TEAM BRASS books. TEAM WOODWIND and TEAM BRASS ensemble can therefore be combined for both small wind/brass groups or for full-sized wind orchestras.

The titles included in the Supplement which accompanies this book can be played in unison, 'thirds' or harmony with the same titles in the CLARINET book. All relevant pieces are fully cross-referenced.

All the ensemble material is graded to match the lesson material. The ensemble pieces may easily be located by following the direction at the foot of the appropriate lesson page. Scores for all ensemble material and more extensive notes appear in the ACCOMPANIMENTS book.

The following symbols have been used to provide an immediate visual identification:

 Pieces with piano accompaniment

 Part of an ensemble arrangement for all C, B flat and E flat instruments (scores included in ACCOMPANIMENTS book)

 Pieces playable by flute and clarinet in unison, 'thirds' or harmony to be found in the supplement with this book.

Because the ensemble pieces provide a meeting point for players who are at various stages of development, these pieces may include technical elements (new notes, rhythms, etc) which are not in fact introduced until some pages later.

Edited by BARRIE CARSON TURNER

Piano accompaniments by GEOFFRY RUSSELL-SMITH and BARRIE CARSON TURNER

Sincere thanks are extended to the following people whose criticism, advice and help in various ways have been invaluable.
KEITH ALLEN, Head of Music Services for the City of Birmingham Education Department.
PHILIP BROOKES, Bassoonist.
PETER BULLOCK, Clarinet Teacher, Derbyshire County Education Department.
RICHARD REAKES, Oboe Teacher, City of Birmingham Education Department.
DAVID ROBINSON, Woodwind Teacher, Kirklees Education Department.
JULIE SCHRODER, Flute Teacher, City of Birmingham Education Department.
ALISON WHATLEY, Oboe Teacher, City of Birmingham Education Department.
And also to the many pupils who have worked with the TEAM WOODWIND books in transcript form.
First Published 1991
Reprinted 1993.

Cover Design: Ian Barrett / David Croft
Cover Photography: Ron Goldby
Production: Stephen Clark / David Croft
Reprographics: Cloverleaf
Instruments photographed by courtesy of Vincent Bach International Ltd., London.

Typeset by Cromwell Typesetting & Design Ltd., London / Printed in England by Halstan & Co. Ltd.

TEAM WOODWIND: Flute
ISBN 0 86359 781 5 / Order Ref: 17531 / 215-2-652

Lesson diary & practice chart

Date (week commencing)	Enter number of minutes practised.							Teacher indicates which pages to study.
	Mon	Tue	Wed	Thur	Fri	Sat	Sun	
1995						/		

Getting Started

The first notes can be played using just the HEAD JOINT of the flute on its own. Experiment with the position of the head joint on the lips until a clear sound is produced. Try playing loud sounds and soft sounds, long sounds and short sounds.

How to put the Flute together

HEAD JOINT   MIDDLE JOINT   FOOT JOINT

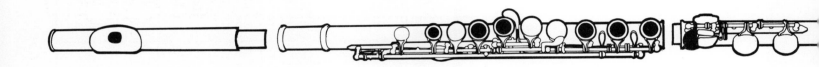

Gently twist the head joint into the middle joint. Then twist the foot joint into the other end of the middle joint. Make sure that the three joints of the flute are lined up as shown below.

How to hold the flute

Left hand fingers

Right hand fingers

Left hand thumb

Look in a mirror to check that you are holding
the flute the way your teacher tells you.

Start with B . . .

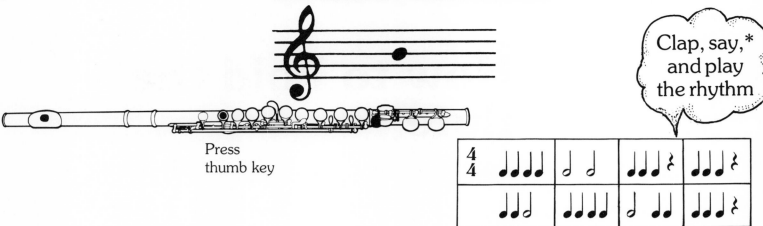

Press
thumb key

Clap, say,*
and play
the rhythm

*French time names may be used.

The TIME SIGNATURE 4/4 means each bar must add up to FOUR beats

A CROTCHET (or QUARTER-NOTE) lasts for ONE beat

A MINIM (or HALF-NOTE) lasts for TWO beats

A CROTCHET REST lasts for ONE beat

A COMMA means take a breath

bar 1   bar 2   bar 3   bar 4

PULSE-clap or beat time

■ This page can be played in 3rds with page 2 in the CLARINET book.

. . . then on to A

Move across, up or down from one box to the next

Press thumb key

BAR LINES divide a line of notes into sets. In $\frac{4}{4}$ time each bar adds up to four crotchet beats

(2 + 1 + 1 = 4)   (1+1+1+1 = 4)

A's and B's

The DOUBLE BAR marks the end of a piece of music

Elegy

Slowly and sadly

This page can be played in 3rds with page 3 in the CLARINET book.

The note G

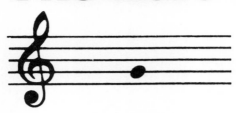

Press
thumb key

G, A and B March

A SEMIBREVE (or WHOLE-NOTE)
lasts for FOUR beats

Merrily we roll along

Traditional

Au clair de la lune

Traditional

Tricky tune

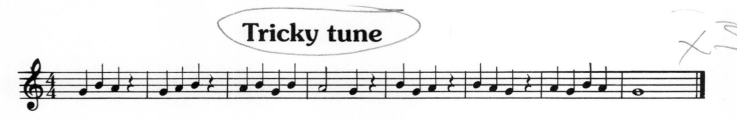

■ Proceed to F on page 6; or C on page 5.

The note C

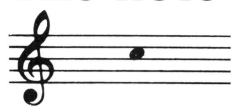

No thumb
key

Flowing

Walking

Sort 'em out!

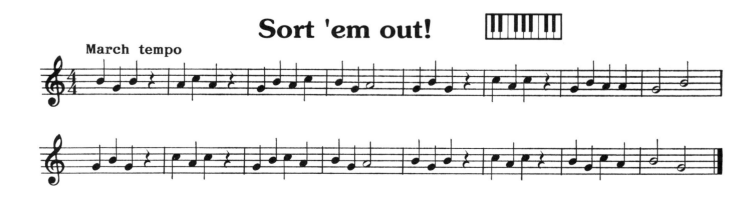

The note F

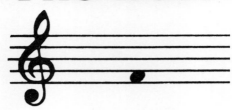

Press
thumb key

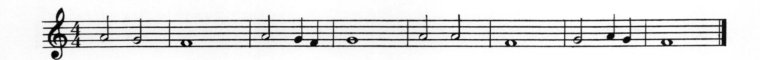

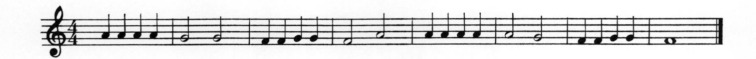

Merrily we roll along

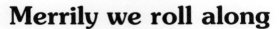

Traditional

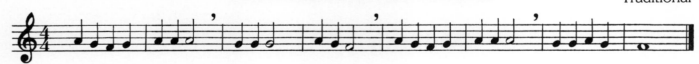

Acapulco Bay

This piece can be played in conjunction with *Acapulco Bay* opposite.

Tempo de beguine

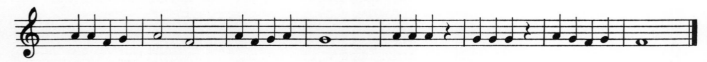

■ Proceed to Low E on page 11; or B♭ on page 7.

The note B♭

Press thumb key

The FLAT lowers the pitch of a note by ONE SEMITONE

'C' means Common Time i.e. $\frac{4}{4}$ time

Ode to joy

LUDWIG VAN BEETHOVEN (1770–1827)

Welsh tune

Traditional

Acapulco Bay

Tempo de beguine

This piece can be played in conjunction with *Acapulco Bay* opposite.

■ For related ensemble material see pages 14 & 15 (upper parts & duets).

The key signature of F major

Alternative B♮ fingering

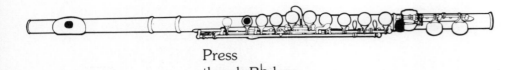

Press
thumb B♮ key

The flat on the middle line makes all the B's flat

B♮

The two dots mean that the music should be repeated

Step round

(1) (2) (3) (4)

Go and tell aunt Rhody

Traditional

play by ear

Brightly

Brightly

Continue

Continue

For related ensemble material see pages 14 & 15.

The note D

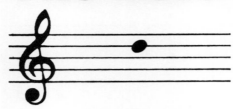

Press
thumb key

Twinkle, twinkle, little star

Round   Traditional

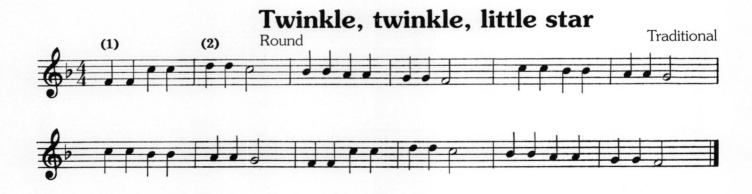

Jazzily

Fast

Low E

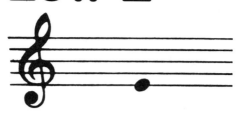

Press
thumb key

Low E with F and G

Low E with F, G and A

One man and his dog

Traditional

■ For related ensemble material see pages 14 & 15; quavers on page 17.

Upper E

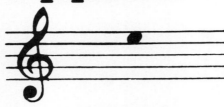

This note has the same fingering as LOW E

Press
thumb key

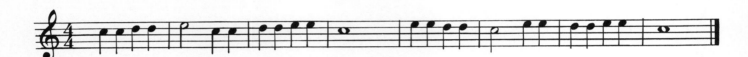

Pattern

Phrase A   Phrase B   Phrase A repeated   Phrase C

Slow round

Slowly   Continue   Merrily   Continue

■ Quavers on page 17; ensemble up to E on page 20 (*Regal fanfare*); Upper F on pages 18 & 19; slurs on page 13.

Slurs

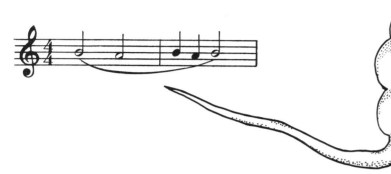

The notes covered by a SLUR are played smoothly and in one breath, with only the first note being tongued

Slur round

Morning

EDVARD GRIEG (1843-1907)

Victorian ballad

German tune
(Descant part with B♭ clarinet/trumpet duet)

Traditional

Lullaby
(Descant part with B♭ clarinet/trumpet duet)

German tune
Duet

Traditional

■ The descant parts above integrate with B♭ ensemble material in the CLARINET and TRUMPET books. Third parts to flute duets are located in the Supplement to the CLARINET book for both Clarinet in B♭ and Clarinet in C.

Canzonetta for flute duet on page 16.

Tied notes

A minim tied to a crotchet lasts for 3 beats

A crotchet tied to a crotchet lasts for 2 beats

A semibreve tied to a crotchet lasts for 5 beats, and so on

Canzonetta

Duet

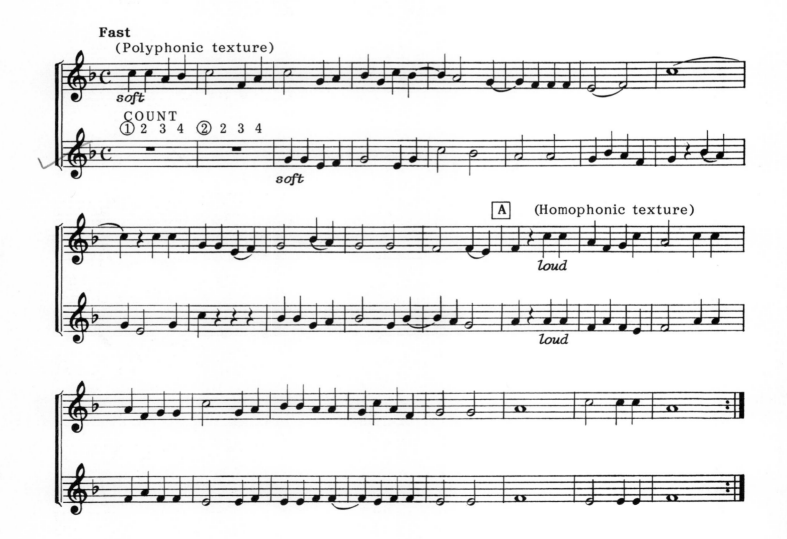

■ Tied notes in $\frac{3}{4}$ on page 19; more tied notes on pages 20, 21, 22, etc.

Quavers

Skip to my Lou

Traditional

Sleigh ride

Related ensemble material on pages 20 & 21; Quavers in $\frac{6}{8}$ on page 35.

Upper F

This note has the same fingering as LOWER F

Press
thumb key

Slowly

Scale and arpeggio of F major

Round the scale

Moderato
(1)   **(2)**

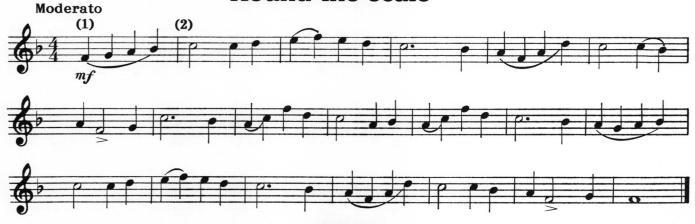

mf

Play by ear

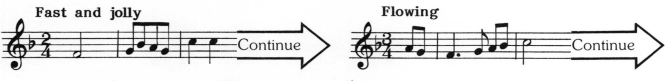

Fast and jolly   Continue   **Flowing**   Continue

■ Proceed to F♯ on page 22; or G on pages 23 & 24; related ensemble material on page 20; related material on page 19.

Westminster chimes

Amazing grace

Traditional

The QUAVER TRIPLET means that three quavers are played in the time of one crotchet

Lasst uns erfreuen

Traditional

Regal fanfare
(Descant part with B♭ clarinet/trumpet trio)

When I first came to this land
(Descant part with B♭ clarinet/trumpet duet)

Traditional

Regal fanfare
Trio

When I first came to this land for flute duet on page 21.

Blowin' in the wind

(Descant part with B♭ clarinet/trumpet duet)

Words and Music
by BOB DYLAN

When I first came to this land

Duet

Traditional

■ *Blowin' in the wind* for flute duet on page 27.

The notes F♯ and upper F♯

Both notes have the same fingering

The SHARP raises the pitch of a note by ONE SEMITONE

Press thumb key

Workin' on the railroad

Like a jolly cowboy saloon song

The sharp, flat or natural sign appearing before a note is called an ACCIDENTAL

Coventry carol

Traditional

Moderato

The NATURAL sign cancels the effect of a sharp or a flat

Upper G

The key
signature
of G major

This note has the same fingering as LOWER G

Press
thumb key

The sharp on the top line makes all the F's sharp

Scale and arpeggio of G major

F♯

Barcarolle

JACQUES OFFENBACH
(1819–1880)

Sing hosanna

Traditional

Edelweiss

From *The Sound of Music*

Words by OSCAR HAMMERSTEIN II
Music by RICHARD RODGERS

Morning has broken

Traditional

Upper A

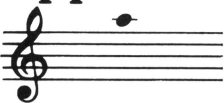

This note has the same fingering as LOWER A

Press
thumb key

Wiegenlied

Traditional

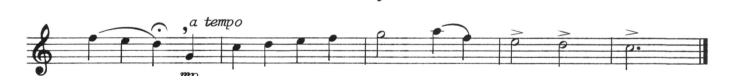

Frère jacques

Traditional

■ Related ensemble material on pages 27 & 37; proceed to High B & C on page 28; or to dotted crotchet/quaver on page 26; or 6/8 time on page 35; or C♯ on page 30.

Dotted crotchets

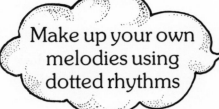

Make up your own melodies using dotted rhythms

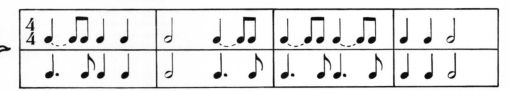

Join the dots to make the dotted-crotchet/quaver effect

ANTONIN DVOŘÁK
(1841–1904)

New World Symphony

Largo

p

Quick march

March tempo

f

Auld lang syne

Scottish traditional

Sentimentally

mf

f

play by ear

Brightly

Continue

Grandly

Continue

■ Dotted quavers on page 32; *Auld lang syne*
for clarinet unison on page 25 in the CLARINET book.

High B

Press
thumb key

High C

No thumb
key

These notes have the same fingerings as LOWER B and C

Scale and arpeggio of C major

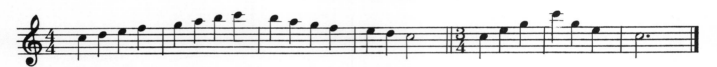

The first Nowell

Traditional

Brightly

Yankee Doodle

Traditional

Sprightly

■ Proceed to High D on page 42; or C♯ on page 30;
or semiquavers on page 31; or dotted quavers on page 32;
or E♭ on page 34.

Pomp and Circumstance
March No. 4

EDWARD ELGAR
(1857–1934)

Love me tender

Words and Music by VERA MATSON
& ELVIS PRESLEY

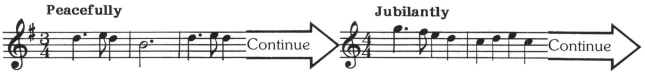

The notes C♯ and High C♯

Both notes have the same fingering

No thumb
key

The key signature of D major

Sing hosanna

Traditional

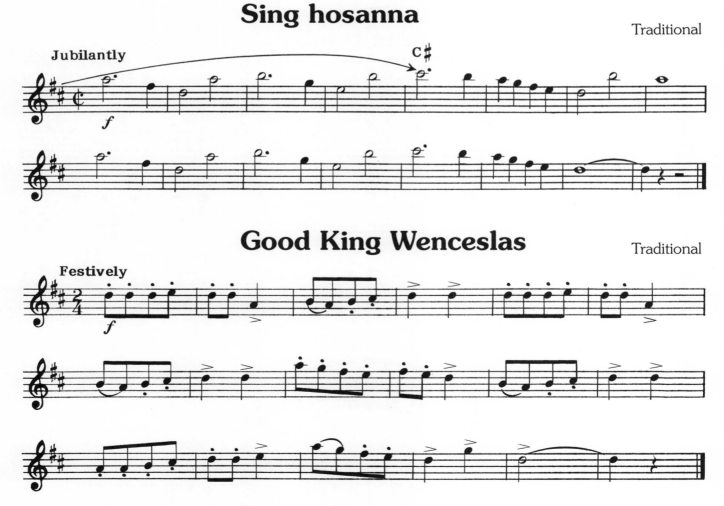

Good King Wenceslas

Traditional

■ Proceed to High D on page 42; or Low D on page 41.

Semiquavers in 2/4

Semiquavers are sometimes
called SIXTEENTH-NOTES

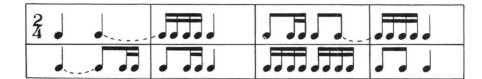

Semiquaver study

Join the dots in order to make
'ties' as and when required

The dotted quaver

Say 'goodbye'

from *The Marriage of Figaro*

WOLFGANG AMADEUS MOZART
(1756–1791)

John Brown's body

Traditional

The old hundredth

Traditional

Maestoso

Polovtsian dance

ALEXANDER BORODIN
(1833–1887)

Lilting, not fast

L'Arlésienne suite No. 1

GEORGES BIZET
(1835–1875)

Allegro deciso

Low E♭

Press
thumb key

Upper E♭

Press
thumb key

Villikins and his Dinah

Traditional

Away in a manger

WILLIAM JAMES KIRKPATRICK
(1838-1921)

Key signature of B♭ major

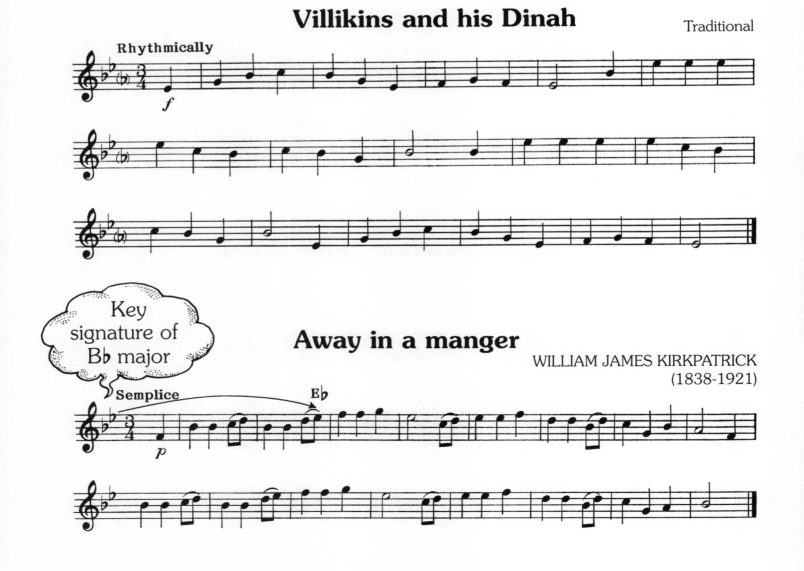

6/8 Time

and its relationship with 2/4 time.

Related ensemble material on page 39; more 6/8 on pages 41 & 54; *When Johnny comes marching home* for Clarinet unison on page 40 in the CLARINET book.

Upper B♭

This note has the same fingering as LOWER B♭

Press
thumb key

Alternative B♭ fingering

Press thumb B♭ key

Scale and arpeggio of B♭ major

Joy to the world

GEORGE FRIDERIC HANDEL
(1685–1759)

Canon

GUSTAV MAHLER (1860–1911)

■ Related ensemble material on page 37.

Au clair de la lune

Traditional

Little donkey

Words and Music by ERIC BOSWELL

Slow down gradually.

Quaver syncopation

To be played:
(a) In strict time
(b) In swing time

West Indian carnival

Fast and jolly

■ Related ensemble material on page 39; more syncopation on pages 43, 52 & 53.

Ab has the same fingering as G# (page 40)

Tijuana brass

The CAUTIONARY ACCIDENTAL reminds you this note is F and no longer F#

I saw three ships

Traditional

The notes G♯ & A♭ and Upper G♯ & A♭

Both notes have the same fingering

G♯ /A♭ key

Press
thumb key

Allegretto

ANTONIO DIABELLI (1781–1858)

The key signature of A major

Canon

THOMAS TALLIS (1505–1585)

■ Relevant ensemble material on page 39 (for A♭).

Low D

Press
thumb key

Three blind mice

Round

Traditional

I gave my love a cherry

Traditional

High D

Press
thumb key

Scarboro' fair

Traditional

Lilting

La basque

MARIN MARAIS (1656–1728)

Con brio

■ Related ensemble material on pages 48 & 49.

Scale and arpeggio of D major

Caribbean dance

Traditional

Tempo di Rumba

f

p

Fine

D.C. al Fine

play by ear

Joyfully

Continue

Caribbean dance for Clarinet unison on page 44 in the CLARINET book.

Low C#

Press thumb key

low C# key

Low C

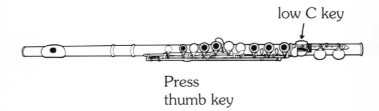

low C key

Press thumb key

The Pink Panther

by HENRY MANCINI

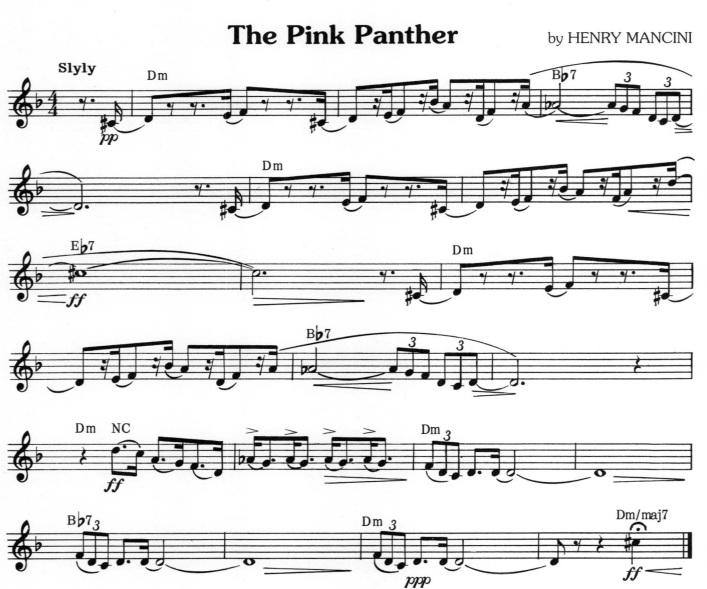

High E

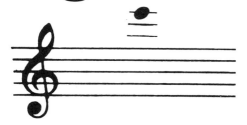

Press
thumb key

Over the rainbow

Words by E. Y. HARBURG
Music by HAROLD ARLEN

■ *Over the rainbow* in unison with Clarinet in the FLUTE
SUPPLEMENT.

High F

Press
thumb key

Romance

WOLFGANG AMADEUS MOZART
(1756–1791)

Chromatics

Chromatic scale of D

Play the scale using different rhythms

Mazurka

FREDERIC CHOPIN (1810–1849)

Michael row the boat ashore

Traditional

Canzona

Part 1

ADRIANO BANCHIERI (1568–1634)

Compose an accompaniment for Tambour using crotchets, quavers and semi-quavers

Canzona

Part 2

O little town of Bethlehem

Traditional

St. Anthony Chorale

JOSEPH HAYDN
(1732–1809)

High F♯

Press
thumb key

High G

No thumb
key

Scale and arpeggio of G major

March

CARL PHILIPP EMANUEL BACH
(1714-1788)

Allegro assai

Berceuse

from *Dolly Suite*

GABRIEL FAURÉ (1845-1924)

Allegretto moderato

High E♭

Press
thumb key

The swinger

Accompaniment for Keyboard on '16 beat' rhythm setting	$\frac{4}{4}$	Bars					
		4	2	2	1	1	2
		F m	B♭ m	F m	C7(−13)	B♭ m	F m
		Chords					

Sweet Georgia Brown

Words and Music
by BEN BERNIE,
KENNETH CASEY &
MACEO PINKARD

The theme (up to *Fine*) can be played in unison with clarinet
version on page 59 in the CLARINET book.

Sicilienne

GABRIEL FAURÉ (1845–1924)

March

from *Judas Maccabaeus*

GEORGE FRIDERIC HANDEL
(1685–1759)

Scales and arpeggios

Scale and arpeggio of F major

Scale and arpeggio of B♭ major

Scale and arpeggio of A major

Scale of A minor harmonic

Arpeggio of A minor

Scale of D minor harmonic

Arpeggio of D minor

Scale of E minor harmonic

Arpeggio of E minor

Scale of B minor harmonic

Arpeggio of B minor

Scale and arpeggio of E♭ major

Scale of F♯ minor harmonic

Arpeggio of F♯ minor

Scale of G minor harmonic

Arpeggio of G minor

Siciliana and allegro

from *Sonata in F*

GEORGE FRIDERIC HANDEL
(1685–1759)

Largo and Minuet

from *Trio in D*

JOHANN QUANTZ
(1697–1773)